Flynn's Last Camp

Flynn's Last Camp

by Maisie McKenzie

PUBLISHED BY BOOLARONG PUBLICATIONS

Other books by Maisie McKenzie:
The Road to Mowanjum
Mission to Arnhem Land
No Town Like Alice

First published in 1985
by Boolarong Publications,
24 Little Edward Street, Spring Hill, Brisbane. Qld.

Copyright © Maisie McKenzie

This book is copyright. Apart from any fair dealing for the purposes of private study, research, criticism or review, as permitted under the Copyright Act, no part may be reproduced by any process without written permission. Inquiries should be addressed to the Publishers.

All rights reserved.

National Library of Australia
Cataloguing-in-Publication data

McKenzie, Maisie.
 Flynn's Last Camp.

ISBN 0 86439 000 9.

1. Flynn, John, 1880-1951. 2. Missionaries – Australia – Biography. 3. Royal Flying Doctor Service of Australia. 4. Presbyterian Church – Missions. I. Title.

266'.5294'0924

BOOLARONG PUBLICATIONS
24 Little Edward Street, Spring Hill, Brisbane. Qld.
Design, reproduction and photo-typesetting by Press Etching Pty. Ltd., Brisbane.
Printed by James Ferguson Pty. Ltd., Brisbane.
Bound by Podlich Enterprises Pty. Ltd., Brisbane.

Maisie McKenzie

This book is dedicated to all those men and women who have striven throughout the years to further the vision and the work of John Flynn in casting a Mantle of Safety over the Australian Inland.

Flynn's Last Camp

It is dawnlight on Mt. Gillen
And soft finger-shadows deep
Over rock and red sand
Over gum and corkwood creep,
Seeking out the hillock
Where John Flynn's ashes sleep.
And I think about the Old Boss,
His dreams, and his concern;
Did he too, like Moses,
See a bush begin to burn,
As he ached for all those battlers
In a land both vast and stern?

It is noonday, but Mt. Gillen
Stands ramrod in the air,
Despite her throbbing temples,
Her flanks, red-hot and bare;
And still she guards the hillock
And the great man resting there.
And I think about the Old Boss,
His doctors in the air,
The bushmen at their pedal sets,
The nursing sisters' care.
And I thank God for the Old Boss
And his ashes resting there.

It is evening, and Mt. Gillen
Is mauve against the sky,
Her shadows reaching downwards
Past the creekbed dry,
Resting on the hillock
Where John Flynn's ashes lie.
Again I see the Old Boss
Communing silently,
And in the gathering darkness
Under Gillen's lea,
I'm conscious of a foretaste
Of God's eternity.

                              M. McK.

Contents

Foreword	ix
'Flynn of the Inland'	1
John Flynn's Grave	11
The Devil's Marbles	24
The MacDonnell Ranges	33
Trail Blazers in the Area	47
A Proud and Ancient Race	54
On the Move in the Centre	62
A Prophet in the Wilderness	68

Foreword

Maisie McKenzie has written a book on 'Flynn of the Inland' that is both informative and fascinating.

Although inspired by his extraordinary grave, her narrative reveals an appreciation of John Flynn as he was in life. More than this, she tells the story behind the grave — of the bush people he served and the harsh country he adopted.

The sight of lonely inland graves always distressed Flynn as they brought home to him the terrible isolation of bush men and women, many of whom died needlessly far from medical help. To Flynn this was a challenge, reinforced whenever he heard tragic stories like that of Bob Currie.

Currie was bringing his young wife from Noranside into Cloncurry to have her child. They were travelling with a spring cart and horses. Monsoonal rains set in and they became bogged down at Rocky Hole, not far from the present day Chatsworth Station. The flooded creek was an impossible barrier.

Elizabeth Currie gave birth to her baby on a blanket in the mud. Bob carted water in a billy can to bathe her with his sweat rag; but both mother and baby died. They were buried together in a quickly dug sodden grave on the banks of Rocky Hole and Bob Currie cut down some mulga saplings for a rough enclosure around the mound of wet earth.

'Is the Church really interested in lonely graves?' Currie angrily asked Flynn. 'Well, you go back and tell 'em!' he said.

With determination, Flynn did tell the Church. Indeed he told parliamentarians, public gatherings, newspaper reporters and ordinary people all over Australia. But he was not content merely to talk — he set out himself to establish a flying doctor service, pedal wirelesses, bush nursing hostels, old timers' homes, and a network of patrolling padres.

Maisie McKenzie not only places John Flynn in his truly national niche, she also makes the resting place of his ashes a focal point of Centralian social history.

My personal association with the planning and construction of the John Flynn Memorial Church in Alice Springs and with the building of the John Flynn Grave, compel me to say that her book tells the real story for the first time. Furthermore, its well planned brevity and warm humanity make it extremely readable.

Fred McKay

Chapter One

'Flynn of the Inland'

'The most important thing in life is to survive failure'
(Flynn's 'Bushman's Companion' 1909)

His Dreaming
Many people dream dreams, but the greatness of John Flynn was that not only did he have the vision, but he flexed his muscles and, with dogged endurance, made it all come true.
  Who was he, this Flynn of the Inland, this man who ended his life with a Devil's Marble on his grave?
  You would not notice him in a crowd, yet this ordinary looking, humble man is acknowledged as one of the 'greats' of Australian history. He was honoured for his community work by the Crown, recognised as a nation-builder by both Federal and State governments, appointed to its highest leadership by the Church, and acclaimed by the people of the outback as their champion.
  Early Life: Flynn was born at Moliagul in Victoria on 25 November, 1880. He matriculated from University High School in Melbourne and his Principal wrote 'John Flynn matriculated within sixteen months . . . This was due to his commendable industry and perseverance, as well as to his intellectual ability. He is one of the most trustworthy, painstaking and upright pupils this school has had for some time.'
  The young Flynn became a pupil teacher for four years, and developed hobbies of photography and First Aid. During these years there was a constant stirring within him to become a minister, and in 1903 he became a Home Missionary in a remote area of Victoria where his First Aid training proved invaluable.

In 1907 he enrolled as a theological student at Ormond College, Melbourne, but 1909 was the year that was a cross-roads in his life. He was shown a letter written by Mrs Jessie Litchfield of Darwin. In the letter she stated in simple terms some of the immense problems of those living in isolation, particularly the lack of the church's presence. 'Why cannot the Presbyterian Church send up a missionary to the N.T. . . . ? she asked.

Flynn was moved by her plea and determined then that his future work would always be in Australia rather than as an overseas missionary. That year he undertook a mission to shearers in western Victoria. It was a great training-ground for Flynn as it was here he became aware of the bush people's need, not only for a pastor, but for information on many practical matters like first aid, what to do at a burial, directions for making a will, etc. So isolated were these people, they even lacked a calendar! And so, the *Bushman's Companion* came into being in 1910 with thousands of copies distributed. This little book, which combined helpful information with Bible selections, hymns and prayers, soon became indispensable to many isolated people.

In 1911, Flynn commenced a two year term with the Smith of Dunesk Mission in South Australia, and there his concern for the people of the outback was deepened even further.

At the age of 32, in 1912, he was delighted to be asked by the Church to undertake a fact-finding journey into inland Australia. He met and talked, sometimes all night, with bush people, men out building stockyards, women in lonely kitchens, drovers, fossickers, men on the track, store folk and officials in tiny settlements.

The more he talked with people, the more he became convinced that, if the Government were doing nothing to alleviate the physical, social and spiritual problems of the lonely battlers on the frontiers of the nation, then it was high time the Church stepped in and played its historic role of fore-runner.

As a result of that conviction, and as an outreach of the then Presbyterian Church, the Australian Inland Mission was born in 1912. Its very name spoke eloquently of Flynn's determination that his task was to be national rather than denominational. Its motto was 'For Christ and the Continent' and this remained in the forefront of planning through the years to come.

Flynn was appointed as first Superintendent of the A.I.M., a position he held through thick and thin for 39 years.

A Mantle of Safety: Flynn conceived an overall plan which he called 'a Mantle of Safety'. It was to cover the whole of the three million square kilometres of outback Australia. During his entire leadership, he never deviated from this vision, despite two world

John Flynn, 1880 — 1951

wars and the devastating economic depression of the thirties. He died having achieved his aim.

It was a task most people believed to be impossible, but his imprint can be seen today throughout the Inland. He cast a very long shadow indeed. In Alice Springs alone, the Hospital, the Flying Doctor Service, the School of the Air, the Country Women's Association of the Air, the John Flynn Memorial Church, Adelaide House (the original nursing home, now a museum), and the Old Timers' Homes are all the practical outcome of this one man's dreaming.

When he died in 1951, his mantle of safety over the inland included a chain of bush hospitals giving medical and social security to nineteen isolated communities; an incredible network of pedal radios linking together numerous distant homes and settlements; the first flying doctor service in the world (known since 1954 as the Royal Flying Doctor Service); welfare clubs for pioneers in newly developing areas; distribution of good literature to outback people; and a scheme of boundary riding patrol padres who travelled into every corner of the Never Never.

While achieving this vision, Flynn never allowed himself to become daunted by failures or disapointments. He literally became a servant of the outback bush folk, overcoming obstacle after obstacle in what he called 'the battle for a brighter bush'. When he died, he had no bank account nor home of his own. His fireside had been beside the track and beyond the farthest fence. His quart pot had been blackened from countless camps amid the mulga and the coolibahs. His music had been the sound of the breeze in the graceful desert oaks, and birdsong at dawn. His bed had been his swag. His companions were the lonely bushmen, the boundary riders, the isolated settlers. A strange man — every inlander's mate with his sleeves rolled up, working beside them in stockyard building, house repairs, digging, mustering; at home in a drover's camp or over a rough table in an outback kitchen, yet equally at ease with Government officials back in the cities as he tried to influence decision-making in favour of the forgotten people of the inland.

Memorials

Moliagul: Many memorials honour John Flynn. At Moliagul, in Victoria, opposite the house in which he was born, is a simple, tall, white column. Alongside it is a plinth of local stonework, including chips of pink and white marble and a piece of red sandstone from Alice Springs. The inscription on the plaque concludes with 'Across the lonely places of the land he planted kindness and gathered love.'

Commemorative Cairn: At the junction of the Barkly and Stuart

Every Inlander's Mate

Highways is another column, rising to a height of 25 feet. This was not built as a memorial to Flynn, for he was still alive at the time of its construction. It was erected by the Flying Doctor Service and was officially known as the John Flynn Commemorative Cairn. It took a lot of persuading to get Flynn to approve of it at all. In the end he agreed only if it would also commemorate the work of those who had helped bring his pedal radio and aerial medical dreams to fulfilment. Its inscription says 'His vision encompassed the continent. He established the Australian Inland Mission and founded the Flying Doctor Service. He brought to lonely places a spiritual ministry and spread a mantle of safety over them by medicine, aviation and radio.'

Cloncurry: Cloncurry in Queensland was the cradle of Flynn's aerial medical and radio work and local residents decided to honour that important part of Australia's history by erecting a memorial. It was here in 1928 that the world's first flying doctor service came into being. The memorial, near the airport, is in the form of a stone obelisk, and the plaque reads ' . . . He brought the Mantle of Safety to the wilderness and solitary places . . . '

An Inland Cathedral: Largest of all the memorials is right in the heart of Alice Springs. This is the John Flynn Memorial Uniting Church in Todd Street. The architect, Arthur Philpot, was surely inspired, for the building is original, interpretative and beautiful.

The builder, James Richards, described his work as the most worthy job of his life. The opening took place on the fifth anniversary of Flynn's death, 5 May, 1956, when the biggest crowd Central Australia had ever seen gathered to dedicate it. Many Australians contributed to the building; cattlemen and wolfram miners gave the entrance pool with its symbolic artesian bore water; a pastoralist donated stringy bark timber for the pews; and others gave symbolic gifts too numerous to recount. The people of the inland felt that it was their tribute to the man who had always dreamed of a 'cathedral' in the centre of Australia. The names of local people like Jimmy Richards, who was killed during the building process, Ted Smith, Bill Traeger, Aussie Richards, D.D. Smith, Johnnie Ronberg, Les Hansen, Reg Harris, Allan Armitage and Aboriginal Bobbie Myers are all inscribed on the building. The quarrying of marble in the Strangways, the shovelling of sandstone at Temple Bar, the individual manufacture on site of thousands of bricks, all were part and parcel of an enterprise which bore the down to earth marks of Flynn himself. 'He spread a mantle of safety over inland Australia' is the tribute on the plaque inside the church.

The A.I.M. Jubilee Stamp: One of the most impressive memorials to Flynn was the issue of a special stamp. In 1962, the Australian Inland Mission celebrated its fiftieth anniversary and the Commonwealth Government honoured Flynn and his work by issuing a jubilee postage stamp. The Prime Minister, Robert Menzies, who had visited Flynn's grave in 1956, suggested that a drawing of it would make an appropriate background for the proposed stamp.

The Post Master General's Department selected Frank Manley of Essendon, Victoria, to undertake the design.

It is a famous stamp, the first in Australia to be produced in four colours by the photogravure process. It features an A.I.M. nursing sister standing in the foreground of Mt Gillen, with John Flynn's grave and the ghost gum in solid relief.

The Stamp was released for public sale on 5 September, 1962. Nine thousand First Day Covers were franked in Alice Springs that day, and several hundreds more in Birdsville, Coen, Oodnadatta and other outback post offices.

In England it was alluded to in the *Philatelic Journal of Great Britain* as a noteworthy pioneering example of the art of photogravure, and in Australia it became a collector's item. Through it the picture of Flynn's grave with its distinctive Devil's Marble, climbed into a memorable place in the history of world-wide postal communication.

A Devil's Marble: The Devil's Marble itself is Flynn's most

James Richards, well known Building Contractor and Stone Mason, voluntarily carried out all the basic construction work on John Flynn's Grave in August 1953. He had come to Alice Springs especially to build the John Flynn Memorial Church which was to be the culminating act of his career. On 16 August, 1955 he was killed in an accidental fall from the high scaffolding in the interior of the building. The whole Alice Springs community gathered at the funeral in tribute to this dedicated and skilled professional builder. His sweat and blood are literally part of the John Flynn Church and his ashes rest in the Pioneers' Wall of Remembrance.

extraordinary memorial; it is what makes his grave unique. And of all people, Flynn would have appreciated the irony of a man of God being honoured in such a way — by a Devil's Marble! On it are inscribed the words 'He brought gladness and rejoicing to the wilderness and the solitary places'.

John Flynn, his life and achievements, live on through these memorials. But the fascination does not stop there. The story behind the grave itself is also part of Australian history.

8   Flynn's Last Camp

Prime Minister Menzies made his first trip to the Northern Territory to set the foundation stone of the John Flynn Memorial Church on 26 June, 1954. Mr Menzies (later Sir Robert) also made a special visit to the Flynn Grave and later gave his personal approval to the production of the A.I.M. Commemorative Postage Stamp which featured 'Flynn's Last Camp'.

Sample of First Day Cover on day of issue of Commemorative Stamp showing Flynn's Grave.

'Flynn of the Inland' 9

Stamp issued by Australian National Government in 1962 to mark 50 years of service by the A.I.M. to the people of the outback. First day covers are available for stamp collectors.

10   Flynn's Last Camp

The grave as it looks today.

Fred McKay reads the inscription on the grave of his "Old Boss".

Chapter Two

John Flynn's Grave

'If you start an idea, nothing can stop it'
(Flynn in a personal letter, 1919)

'This is where I would like to be buried'
John Flynn's first sight of Alice Springs was from the back of a camel. He gazed around him and, at the sight of the long sweep of the ancient MacDonnell Ranges, he felt an overwhelming sense of belonging.

Forty years later, when he stood on jutting Mt Gillen for the last time, he still had that same uplifting of his spirit. Here beat the heart of the land he loved. He felt, like the Aborigines, that he was part of it. His sweat was in the red sand. He had rejoiced in it, wept over it, been frustrated and inspired by it.

Now, with growing frailty of body, he stood in quiet wonder on Gillen's rugged spur. He looked down at the sandy bed of winding Chinaman Creek; at the ghost gums and corkwoods; at the red rocks and ever changing colours of the hills; at the old road winding westward — that road he knew so well, for it was there that the pedal wireless experiments had taken place.

'This is where I would like to be buried', he said.

And so it happened that, on 5 May, 1951, when the newspaper billboards all over Australia made the solemn three word announcement 'Flynn is Dead', his inland friends planned to carry out his wish.

His death had come suddenly, but peacefully, in Prince Alfred Hospital, Sydney, a few months before his seventieth birthday, after 39 arduous years working on the frontiers of this land. The main funeral ceremony was conducted in St Stephen's Church,

John Flynn, at 71 years of age, his dreams realised, sitting at his desk in his Sydney Office. This picture was taken by the Sydney Morning Herald a few months before Flynn died, and is probably the last photograph taken of him as he was preparing for retirement. Suddenly stricken with abdominal cancer, and after a very short illness in Royal Prince Alfred Hospital Sydney, he 'went to be with his fathers' at 3 p.m. on Saturday 5 May, 1951.

opposite Parliament House in Sydney on 9 May, 1951. A simple cremation service followed. His ashes were then flown to Alice Springs by the Commonwealth Government in a special DC3 aircraft, so that his friends of the inland could bid him the last farewell.

Memorial services were conducted all over Australia and tributes paid to him by people from all walks of life. Perhaps one that would have appealed to him most came from an old-timer at Hatches Creek in the Northern Territory. He said simply 'John Flynn put hobbles on the bush'.

The Interment in Central Australia

Thursday 23 May, 1951 was an unforgettable day in the Centre. All shops were closed in Alice Springs. The District Engineer, David Smith, a small man with wiry stature and the heart of a lion, got quickly to work and, with teams of men, graded and watered the dusty five kilometre track leading westwards towards Chinaman Creek at the foot of Mt Gillen.

A semi-trailer, parked out in the open, was the platform, draped with flowers that had come from all over Australia. Graham Pitts from the Flying Doctor Radio Base transported a Traeger Transceiver on the back of a utility truck and rigged aerial wires

Flynn's ashes were flown to Alice Springs and a service of committal was conducted on Thursday 23 May, 1951 about 400 metres from the hillock where the present grave site was selected by Mrs Flynn. This was one of Central Australia's historic days and almost all the population of Alice Springs and beyond gathered under the open skies.

14 Flynn's Last Camp

over the top branches of a nearby ghost gum. In this way the entire service was relayed to hundreds of distant homesteads and camps where men, women and children, black and white, listened in reverent silence.

The service was a historic happening for the outback community. Almost the whole population of Alice Springs gathered at the site. Cattlemen and their families made long journeys by night to be there. A truck load of miners in working clothes, came from Hatches Creek. Old Timers from the bush brought out their white shirts and donned them. A group of Aranda Aborigines drove in from Hermannsburg. Church dignitaries flew in from capital cities. Patrol padres turned up in their best suits, A.I.M. Nursing Sisters in their white uniforms, children in school and college clothes for it was school holiday time. And the Northern Territory Police Troopers formed a guard of honour.

Rev. Kingsley (Skipper) Partridge, decked out in unaccustomed Geneva gown and hood, conducted the interment ceremony. Skipper Partridge had been Flynn's patrol padre in that area for many years. He had shared in the struggles, disappointments and

It was a solemn moment as Skipper Partridge stepped down from the dais and placed Flynn's ashes in the very earth where he had served and sweated.

victories and he loved John Flynn as his own father. In a letter to Flynn's widow, Jean, he said that both past and present padres regarded her husband as 'the best Boss ever a man had'.

Skipper Partridge stood on the rustic platform, eyes blinking against the bright light, and spoke with controlled emotion. 'There was a man sent from God, whose name was John' he said quietly. Skipper did not set out to preach a sermon that day, but to paint an unforgettably robust picture of Flynn the man. He spoke simply about Flynn's gentle character, the man who gave unstinted love to the people of the outback, and who, in return, received their unstinted love. 'Here he dreamed his dreams under many a starlit sky' said Skipper. 'Here he worked with pride and joy in a task well done. So here he lies where he longed to be. He is not dead; his work abides; his memory is for ever eloquent. For across the lonely places of the land he planted kindness, and from the hearts of those who call those places home, he gathered love.'

Sun-tanned men, with their riding boots, their bushmen's hats, their erect backs and far-seeing eyes, were not ashamed that day to let the world see their tears.

Gwen Windle, one of the pioneering A.I.M. Nursing Sisters of Alice Springs, was at the pedal organ on the improvised dais. As the words of the final hymn were being sung — 'shine through the gloom and point me to the skies', a Flying Doctor aircraft came in from the north and dropped a wreath of spinifex and roses on the peak of Mt Gillen. Pilot Ian Leslie was at the controls, and each time he flew over the red range, the plane formed the shadow of a cross upon the rocky face. The crowd looked up in silence, awed by the appropriateness of the symbol. The only sound, other than the humming of the plane's engine, was the sudden screeching of some galahs, disturbed into flight from the gums on the bank of the creek.

After the ceremony, the crowd reluctantly dispersed, the sun turned the hills to purple, the evening breeze sighed, and Mt Gillen took over the night watch.

The Gravestone — A Devil's Marble

The site where Flynn's ashes were interred that day was only a provisional one, awaiting a more permanent resting place. The small cairn of ashes was later placed in a fire-proof safe in the Public Works Department office until the grave-proper was constructed on a hillock at the foot of Mt Gillen. The Northern Territory Director of Lands surveyed this area, and it was defined as a Historical Reserve, to be known in perpetuity as 'John Flynn's Grave'. The Reserve is registered officially as containing 0.4376 hectares of land, five kilometres west of Alice Springs, beside the

16 *Flynn's Last Camp*

road which leads westwards, with the spur of Mt Gillen in the background.

When Flynn had mused 'This is where I would like to be buried', he probably didn't give a thought to whether or not his wish would be fulfilled. He would have been moved to see how his friends set about making sure his grave would be like no other in Australia. To use one of his own typical phrases, the whole project had 'the smell of the bush'.

It was left to Rev. Fred McKay, who succeeded John Flynn as the next Superintendent of the Australian Inland Mission, to plan the grave. The inspiration to use a Devil's Marble as the gravestone is credited to David Smith, the District Engineer who said, 'John Flynn's grave should be a bushman's grave. There should be nothing like it anywhere else. Why can't we get one of the Devil's Marbles?'

The Devil's Marbles — giant granite boulders near Barrow Creek, 400 kilometres from where David Smith stood making the suggestion!

But the idea caught on and gained momentum. It was discussed with Jean Flynn, John's widow who was enthusiastic. 'Jack would certainly like that,' she said smiling, knowing how well he would have appreciated both the honour and the irony.

Fred McKay flew to Darwin. He talked with Frank Wise, the Commonwealth Government's Administrator in the Northern Territory. He too was enthusiastic, declaring that he believed if

'Why can't we get one of the Devils Marbles?' asked David Smith. The Devil's Marbles, after millions of years of weathering and erosion by sand, wind and rain, stand like mysterious immovable sentinels on the Stuart Highway 400 kilometres north of Alice Springs.

any man deserved a Devil's Marble for his gravestone, it was John Flynn! In his later retirement in Perth, Wise diarised the interview he had with Fred McKay on 7 March, 1952. 'As the Queen's representative,' he wrote, 'I gave my approval to the use of a boulder (from the Devil's Marbles) as a memorial to Flynn . . . '

An Australian Inland Mission team — Fred McKay, Skipper Partridge and Jack Reynolds — packed their swags and headed north up the track towards the Devil's Marbles. They camped on the site, always an eerie experience with the moonlight casting deep shadows, and the light of the campfire playing on the rocks. In the daylight they wandered up and down among the hundreds of rounded granite boulders strewn in scattered heaps, like huge stone marbles, across the main road and as far as the eye could see. The main problem was to locate a rock suitable in size and location for loading and transportation back to Alice Springs.

Finally they decided on an eight tonne, cylindrically shaped tor, over on the far eastern flank of the area. It was perched on top of a series of other onion-weathered boulders. There was just enough space for George Nichols, of the Public Works Department, to reverse his low-loader to a position where the stone was able to be gradually winched aboard.

Nichols volunteered his services, for he was one of the many who had cause to thank Flynn for his practical vision. After a truck accident in 1935, Nichols was treated in the A.I.M. Nursing

George Nichols, on right, bringing the Devil's Marble.

Home in Alice Springs, and when tetanus threatened, the medical team literally saved his life. So he gladly expended a tremendous physical effort in getting that boulder on to his low loader.

There were no brass bands on the road, no police escort for the big load. The few vehicles met on the way stopped with a screeching of brakes, while the drivers stared back in astonishment as they saw the giant boulder trundling down the track. And as it passed through the small settlements of Wauchope, Barrow Creek, Ti Tree and Aileron, people scratched their heads and rubbed their eyes, scarcely believing what they were seeing.

But when Bill Heffernan of Ti Tree Station learned why the Devil's Marble was on the move, he exclaimed 'He's done it again. John Flynn's resting place will be part of us all.' And that was the common sentiment of the Centralian Old Timers as they watched George Nichols unload the Marble at Chinaman Creek. They felt that, even after his death, their mate, Flynn of the Inland, was still close by, caring and sharing. They felt too, that this lonely grave was somehow just right, for again and again Flynn used to pull up his utility and climb out whenever he saw a grave out in the bush. He knew that each of these graves had a story to tell — the story of a battle lost against hunger or thirst, against sickness or accident, against desperate isolation. So it seemed appropriate that his grave too should be out here in the bush — a symbol that the battle against isolation had at last been won.

There were no architectural working drawings made for the proposed structure of the grave. Mr James Richards, who was later to build the John Flynn Memorial Uniting Church in Alice Springs — and be killed on the job — was an old time stone mason, and he pencilled a drawing on a piece of cardboard, then set about his voluntary task of construction with gads and trowels. Fred McKay, and his son Bruce, carted the quartzite stone from Heavitree Gap and acted as assistant labourers under Jim Richards.

A week later, on 12 August, 1953, the Devil's Marble was moved on to the stone base containing the ashes, and it rested there like a proud sentinel. Jock Pearson of Hastings Deering, Kurt Johannsen, and D.D. Smith were all there with trucks, cranes and lifting gear. Lionel Whittaker and Glen Thomas of the Works Department supervised the movement. All these men in their khaki overalls, and with the sweat dripping from their brows, represented the gratitude of all citizens of the outback in the strange and untrumpeted drama of that final day. It was a tense time, for anything could have happened as that eight tonne boulder swung in mid-air. But at three o'clock, with three cranes

The task of hoisting the 'Devil's Marble' into position on Flynn's grave.
'anything could have happened . . .'

working together as one, the Marble was finally lowered on to the plinth.

There was no account for wages, nor for compensation for working long hours in the scorching sun. Every one there felt a debt to John Flynn, the man who had made the bush safe for them. They stood back and looked at the result of their hard work. There, on the grave, weathered and unadorned rested one of nature's marbles; and they felt that no stone of human fashioning could more majestically guard the ashes of their friend. They went to their homes with a feeling of a job well done. They had that day inscribed a historic landmark on the map of Australia.

Mrs Margaret McKay came back again into the A.I.M. Nursing Team in 1953–54 and voluntarily undertook the matronship of the Bush Mother's Home (Adelaide House) at that critical period when it was been threatened with closure for economic reasons. She was a participant in the whole drama connected with the completion of Flynn's Grave and provided food and drink for the workmen on the site.

John Flynn's Grave 21

'Yes, it is just right'. Mrs Jean Flynn was present on 12 August, 1953 when the Devil's Marble was hoisted into position.
This picture of Mrs Flynn was taken by Trish, a well known photographer in Alice Springs at that time.

22 Flynn's Last Camp

The Jean Flynn Plaque
Mrs Jean Flynn's ashes were flown to Alice Springs and interred
beside those of her husband on 14 November, 1976. The Jean Flynn
Plaque is on the reverse side of the Grave facing southward, and is
affixed to a slab of red sandstone at the base of the quartzite plinth.

When the cranes and trucks had moved away, and the dust had settled, when the silence of the bush descended once more, Mrs Jean Flynn, who had been quietly sitting in the dappled shade of a gnarled corkwood tree, stood up and moved over to the grave, 'Yes,' she said, 'it is just right.'

Two decades later, on 14 November, 1976, Jean Flynn's ashes were also laid to rest within the same grave. Fred Baird, Jean's nephew, who worked with Qantas, the airways company which had provided the first Flying Doctor plane for Flynn, constructed two specially designed stainless steel caskets to contain the ashes of these two great Australians. The caskets were embedded permanently, along with historic records, within the base structure of the grave.

Chapter Three

The Devil's Marbles

'There are sermons in stone and good in everything'
(Shakespeare)

A Natural Wonder

The Devil's Marbles must surely take their place amongst Australia's wonders. To see them for the first time is a startlingly new experience. They loom up suddenly — hundreds and hundreds of giant granite boulders, set against a desert of red sand and rounded clumps of spinifex, on each side of the black slash of bitumen that links Alice Springs with Darwin. They cover an area of 1,828 hectares, near Wauchope, some seventy kilometres south of Tennant Creek.

It is not to be wondered at that they are such a distinctive attraction for visitors to the north. Some of the boulders are as much as twelve metres in diameter; some are perched precariously on top of others, looking like so many gigantic bread rolls; some have been split cleanly in two as if by some mighty axe from the nether regions. It is said that this splitting can occur when there are dramatic and sudden changes in temperature, and the resulting sound is like gun shots echoing through the area. Always there seems to be an air of mystery hovering over the region.

In the day time, when the hot Centralian sun blazes down on them, it is easy to imagine dinosaurs and other pre-historic creatures ambling amongst the great shapes. At night time, however, when the rounded boulders seem to loom even larger, and any stray winds howl more mournfully than a dingo, the Marbles become like something from outer space. Yet there is a

The Devil's Marbles

'This is the Devil's country; he's even emptied his bag of marbles around the place!'

26   *Flynn's Last Camp*

quality about them that attracts like a magnet. Could they talk, they would tell some fantastic stories, tales of the long ago before even Aboriginal man set his foot on our northern shores. Was there anyone here before the Aborigines? Was there any life here millions of years ago? The Marbles could tell us, but they keep their secrets.

It would be difficult to imagine anyone driving past on their way up or down the Track without stopping and wondering how those massive boulders with their curious name got there. Or what the Aboriginal people must have made of them.

HOW THEY GOT THERE

According to geologists, the Marbles are the final product resulting from the cooling off of a molten mass some 1,600,000,000 years ago! The original granite body from which the Marbles were formed, seems to have had three sets of upright joints or planes. The granite gradually broke along these joint lines. Then down through millions of years, winds blew through the joints, rains eroded them, and a chemical flaking of surface-crust reduced the enormous blocks to the myriad shapes we see

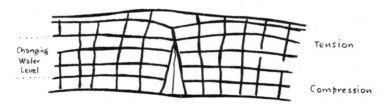

DIAGRAMMATIC SKETCH OF SECTION OF ORIGINAL GRANITE MASS

SKETCH ILLUSTRATING HOW DEVIL'S MARBLES BEGIN TO DEVELOP

SKETCH ILLUSTRATING FINAL STAGES OF WEATHERING PROCESS

How the Devil's Marbles developed over millions of years

today. As the boulders rounded, they fell, or rolled, from their original platforms and became scattered over the area, looking like a game of marbles being played by some race of Colossans.

From the air, one is struck by the touch of man in this otherwise pre-historic looking landscape; for there, running through the centre of the Devil's Marbles, is the Stuart Highway with its rumbling road trains, its caravans, its commercial travellers, its road repair men, hitch-hikers, tourists — up to the minute modern men and women moving through the ancient tors that unfold the geology of millions of years.

Early Explorers and Origin of Name
By rights, John McDouall Stuart should have been the first white man to set eyes on the Devil's Marbles and put them on the map of Australia when he crossed the continent from south to north in 1862, or even when he had got as far as Attack Creek in 1860. His diaries were meticulous, and as there is no mention of the extraordinary boulders, it can only be assumed that he must have passed the area to the west.

So it fell to the lot of John Ross, a rugged Scottish bushman, to make the discovery. Ross was appointed in 1870 as leader of a survey team for the route of the Overland Telegraph line, to be erected between Adelaide and Darwin. He followed McDouall Stuart's tracks, but going more easterly from Barrow Creek, came across the astonishing sight of the immense rounded granite boulders. The team had been travelling for days through dry and forbidding country, and Ross made the jocular comment: 'This is the Devil's country; he's even emptied his bag of marbles around the place!'

The name stuck, and the Devil's Marbles have been on the map ever since.

Another pioneering spirit whose work took him to the Devil's Marbles early this century, was Robert Bruce Plowman, John Flynn's first patrol padre. Bruce Plowman's patrol must surely have been one of the largest parishes in the world, for he covered all the country between Oodnadatta in South Australia and Tennant Creek in the Territory. He travelled by camel, with Dick Gillen, an Aborigine, as his helper — a man he described as 'the best mate' a fellow could have. The adventures Plowman had on those long, lonely stretches, the colourful characters he met in camps, on the track and in isolated homesteads are retailed in his classic book, 'The Man from Oodnadatta'.

In this book he describes his lonely and dangerous journey north through uncharted country in 1914. At Barrow Creek, he rested his camels and met Frank, the Overland Telegraph station operator there. His description of Frank as the 'very essence of virile, competent, Australian manhood' makes it seem as if postal employees today have rather a soft time!

A wonderful type was the short, rotund, elderly little man, illustrative of the kind of men that the bush turns out. Competent and businesslike in the affairs of his department, he was also an extraordinarily good cook and housekeeper in a land where there were no white women. He was his own blacksmith, wheelwright, and carpenter; shod his own horses; mended his own carts and buggy; and built his own sheds as they were needed.

A remarkably good shot . . . he could drop a bullock with a shot through its spinal cord at the coupling of the neck. His own butcher, he skinned and dressed the bullocks he killed.

Equally at home on horse or camel he could ride all day and do the work of a stockman or a camel-driver. As Protector of Aborigines for his district . . . he moved among them unafraid. His influence made the locality safe, to a large extent, for other white men.

In the city he was as much at home as in the bush, and as independent as any townsman. A shrewd wit, a keen judge of men, an all-round efficient competent sort, he flaunted neither his virtues nor his weaknesses, and carried himself with straightforward simplicity.

No wonder Flynn and his patrol padres would stay up all night yarning with courageous, pioneering men like this.

Plowman tells of the difficulties he had of getting reliable directions when he wanted to cut across country with his camels. On this particular occasion, after he had gone 180 kilometres to Hatches Creek wolfram mines on leaving Barrow Creek, he wanted directions back in a northerly direction towards Tennant Creek. After several adventures he came on the Devil's Marbles and recorded that the extraordinary sight overwhelmed him. He was filled with awe as he gazed at the spectacle for the first time, impressed by the 'astonishing disorder of this remarkable array of mighty rocks and boulders.' He tethered his camels and wandered amongst the mammoth stones, feeling like either the first or the last man on earth. Little did he know then that 42 years later he would stand by one of these same marbles at the graveside of his beloved chief, John Flynn.

This was when Plowman came to Alice Springs for the opening of the John Flynn Memorial Uniting Church in 1956. A great company of people made a pilgrimage out to the grave on Sunday afternoon, 7 May, to honour Flynn. Pastor F.W. Albrecht of Hermannsburg Aboriginal Mission, gave an open-air address, 'This great stone, this Devil's Marble, is a symbol which has special meaning for us all in this country,' he said. 'It speaks to us of Flynn's stone-like determination to fulfil his special Christian task, while others thought he was just dreaming.'

Significance of the Devil's Marbles to Aborigines

The late Professor T.C.H. Strehlow, of the University of Adelaide, in speaking of the Devil's Marbles, said: 'Here indeed is natural, unspoiled beauty at its primitive, starkest best . . . cutting across the landscape, creating an illusion of having been built by some Dreamtime mythical ancestor determined, at all costs, to preserve the secrets of their antiquity and guard them forever against the inquisitive intruder.'

Professor Strehlow could have been speaking for the Aborigines, except that to them it would be no illusion. Geology — or any other science for that matter — had no part in their culture, for their race was forced to weave a different strand in the tapestry of humankind. Their understanding of the formation of the Marbles belonged in another dimension altogether, for they believed that it was indeed their spirit ancestors who were responsible for these rocks, and for every other natural feature of the earth's surface.

When Bruce Plowman pulled up his camels amongst the Marbles, he saw no sign of any Aboriginal people. Not far away, at Bonney Creek, dark faces had suddenly emerged and just as suddenly disappeared, but here at the Marbles, not even campfire smoke was visible. Yet doubtless they would have been in the shadows somewhere, seeing wihout being seen, merging with the land as only they seem able to do.

Professor W. Baldwin Spencer and Mr F.J. Gillen were the first anthropologists to make contact with the Aborigines of that district. Both were keen observers and gained invaluable knowledge of the Central Australian tribes. Their books, 'The Native Tribes of Central Australia' and 'The Northern Tribes of Central Australia' are still works that are very highly regarded even today. The two men were so well accepted by the various groups of Aborigines in Central Australia that they, like Strehlow later, were invited to watch many of the sacred ceremonies — a privilege accorded very few white people.

The traditional owners of the Devil's Marbles site are the people of the Kaytej tribe (sometimes spelt Kaititj). It was their men who, on a February night in 1874, slipped through the darkness and speared two white men, James Stapleton and John Franks. These two men were postmaster and linesman, attached to the lonely repeater station on the Overland Telegraph Line at Barrow Creek — the same station where Bruce Plowman had met Frank, the versatile operator. After the attack on Stapleton and Franks, a punitive party was sent out and some seventy Aborigines shot in retribution. The Kaytej people living near the Marbles today are this same tribe.

It is not so very long since they were a desert-dwelling, nomadic people, but massacre and subsequent disasters like drought and disease made such survival impossible. In 1928, a really fierce drought that had devastated the country for four years, made the traditional water-holes a flash-point between the two races. The Aborigines considered the watering places theirs. They had been in their possession for thousands of years, and they resented the white men taking them over for their cattle. The crisis came when a white man, Frederick Brooks, was speared at Coniston Station, south-west of the Marbles. This was followed by the wounding of a second man at Lander River. Severe reprisals resulted in wholesale killings. Official records state that 31 Aborigines were killed, but the way the Aborigines tell it, many more lives were lost. Genealogical studies by anthropologists confirm their higher estimation. In any event, the Coniston massacre of 1928 was so horrendous that the local tribes were forced to scatter. Many of them reluctantly turned to, or were escorted to, the white-managed Aboriginal settlements in Central Australia.

Warrabri became the nearest government reserve to the Devil's Marbles, and the Kaytej people gradually gathered there, along with three other tribal groups — the Warlpiri, the Warramunga and the Alyawarra.

When the Aboriginal Land Rights (N.T.) Act became law in 1976, Aborigines became owners of their Reserve lands. According to anthropologist Diane Bell*some Aboriginal families then left Warrabi, but the Kaytej, traditional owners of the land around the Devil's Marbles, remained there.

In 1983, a further claim was made to the High Court by the Warramunga and Alyawarra tribes for more land. The Devil's Marbles area came into question, but it was proved to be alienated Crown Land, and therefore could not be claimed.

Karlukarlu is the Aboriginal name for the area, and Diane Bell*writes that it is rich in Dreaming sites and ancestral activity. It is a centre for Rain Dreaming, which is not surprising, for this is a semi-arid area, where rain is always precious. When it does come the wilderness is transformed. The wild figs, hanging tenaciously from cracks in the rocks, take on new life. Pools of water gather in the hollows. Grass grows vividly green against the red sand. Wild flowers bloom in abandoned profusion, as if this might be their last opportunity, and the desert becomes a delight with wild fuschia, cassias, acacias, everlasting daisies, pea flowers, billy buttons, wild tomato, pussytails and other colourful flora. But, most important of all, after rain food is there in abundance — food for game and food for gathering.

---

*'Daughters of the Dreaming' (George Allen and Unwin 1983)

So it is easy to believe that the Devil's Marbles is an area of significance to the Aboriginal people. Although there is no evidence of Aboriginal art in the form of rock carvings, or paintings, the Kaytej women say they can still hear the old people crying from the caves, crying for the old way of life that can never come again.

Thus, the Devil's Marbles have come to mean different things to different people. For the Aborigines, they are inextricably bound in their history and in their Dreaming. To the geologist they tell a story that goes back millions of years. To the tourist they are a source of awe and wonder. It seems symbolic that the one that guards John Flynn's ashes serves as a link between the beginning of the Australian continent, long before any black or white footprints were on our shores, and with modern history created by the man who rests there, Flynn of the Inland.

Chapter Four

The MacDonnell Ranges

'There is a sense of spiritual and geographical sweetness in immensity'
(Flynn, 'A.I.M. Land' 1920)

Flynn's First Visit

John Flynn first visited the tiny township of Alice Springs in 1913. Only a handful of white people lived there then, the population estimated at five white women, twenty white men, three families with children and many Aborigines. The railway ended at Oodnadatta in those days, and from there a coach travelled to Horseshoe Bend. From the Bend, the mail was carried by camel, one team going east at 160 kilometres to Alice Springs and the gold mining camps at Arltunga, and the other heading west to the mission station at Hermannsburg.

Flynn's first sight of the MacDonnells was from the back of a camel. This was one of his few experiences of travelling by camel.

There were four camels in the team, led by cameleer Texas, the mailman, who is still remembered in Alice Springs today. The second camel was loaded with mail and attached by a line from its nosepeg to the leading camel's tail. The third, similarly attached to the second, was laden with packs, canteens and general cargo. On top of this load, curled up comfortably, rode Tex's dog, Pup. Pup had burnt his feet on the hot sand on a previous trip, and now enjoyed riding the human way. Flynn was mounted on the fourth camel in the line, together with his quart pot, waterbag, swag and blankets.

Four days of unaccustomed riding on the back of an ungainly, rocking camel, covering only 40 kilometres a day, do not spell

John Flynn, at 33 years of age, when he first rode a camel into Alice Springs with Texas the mailman. This picture was taken in Adelaide before he left.

out luxury, but John Flynn was enthralled by the vast wilderness of the country, and its stark beauty. There was a feeling of unreality when the sun danced on worn shining stones, creating a mirage effect. It felt as if that small party were the only living creatures in a boundless world. His respect for the camels was heightened as they plodded on regardless through the clumps of prickly spinifex that dotted the red sand like so many porcupines. And he treasured the fact that out here 'nobody need worry about talking unless he has something to say. Only the elect can understand the joy of it.' There was time to think out there in the desert. Here and there was a stand of desert oaks, graceful trees giving deep and welcome shade in a hot land and the only sound as they travelled was the swishing of the waterbags as they swung in rhythm with the camels' stride.

However, on the second night out, the rigours of the journey caught up with Flynn and he was sick — camel sick. Tex's remedy was unique and drastic — a diet of raw onions, dry toast and salt, followed by pineapple syrup. Flynn's theory was that the sickness gave up in despair!

But sickness was forgotten on the fourth day when they reached the MacDonnell Ranges. Flynn felt like Milton's 'stout Cortez' when he stared about him with wonder 'silent upon a peak in Darien'. He looked north to the small cluster of buildings that was Alice Springs township, with its hills beyond, to the east and west, where the Ranges greeted him in shades of blue, pink and purple, south where the nearest large city was 1,600 kilometres away over a vast expanse of desert country. He was spellbound by the great drama that Nature unfolded before him, and he felt his own insignificance against this backdrop. He thought about the goal that lay before him, and wondered if he would be strong enough to achieve his vision of a mantle of safety over the people battling in this wilderness.

Perhaps this was the very time when the spirit of John Flynn became one with the spirit of the land. Perhaps, like the Aborigines, this was his link back through the ages to some unknown past. Perhaps he was experiencing a white man's Dreaming.

Although he would have felt the importance of the moment, he could not have known then just how important a part this country was to play both in his life and in his death. This place he had come to was to be the testing ground of many of his dreams and plans. It was to be his wilderness experience, the scene of great heights and great depths. This was where he would cut ironwood posts for the limepits when the Alice Springs nursing home was built. This was where his heart would stand in his mouth as he wondered if the wireless experiment would be a success. This was where his dream of an 'inland cathedral' for the people of the Centre would be realised, even if posthumously. And this would be the place where he would have his last camp — a grave with a Devil's Marble on it.

But this was all to come. At present all he knew was that the struggle would be great, but that his heart beat in tune with the heartland of Australia.

His camel trudged on over those last few kilometres, and John Flynn experienced a feeling of awe that was both physical and spiritual. He had put out his hand and touched the very heart of the country he had come to serve.

36   Flynn's Last Camp

In 1918 when John Flynn took up two allotments of land in Todd Street he said that one day Alice Springs would have 'an inland cathedral' broadcasting church services throughout inland Australia.

The Road West

Flynn's sense of belonging never diminished with the passing years. He came to know the Ranges as well as any bushman, especially the road leading west from the Alice. Whenever he had one of his many baffling problems to struggle with, he found he could think more clearly out here in the uncluttered space of the Ranges than in a noisy city office. There was peace in the agelessness of the worn down hills and the silence that had brooded for over 300 million years. Here he discovered the difference between solitude and loneliness. He found, like others before and since, that being in this country was like a voyage of discovery into one's own soul.

One of Flynn's great satisfactions was to visit the gaps, gorges and chasms of the MacDonnells, always armed with his camera. He was an expert and enthusiastic photographer — a hobby he had pursued since his early days as a teacher in Victoria. Amongst many others taken in the Ranges, is a series of historic photographs at Simpson's Gap. Some of these depict the gums that have a profound spiritual significance to the Aranda people of the Goanna totem, for they believe that these trees mark an important route take by their Goanna ancestors back in the Dreaming.

Like the present day camera enthusiasts, Flynn used to stand in Standley Chasm waiting for the breathless moment when the midday sun would strike the walls of the narrow, red-sided canyon. He didn't have colour-film, nevertheless his pictures are graphic. He delighted in capturing the shapes of gnarled old corkwoods and graceful desert oaks, of cobwebs glistening with dew in the early mornings, of ancient palms and cycads in hidden

Across the distance to Mt Gillen. A John Flynn photograph taken in 1926.

valleys, of mysterious water-holes, of picturesque rock formations, and of the everlasting hills.

These photographs, many on rare glass negatives, are today part of an archival collection, housed in Australia's National Library in Canberra.

The 'Do or Die' Track

That road west through the Ranges became a kind of holy highway for Flynn during the most critical period of his pioneering work. In a way it became a cross-road in his life, for it was here that he would either go forward, or else have his 'mantle of safety' dream blown away like dust in a willy willy.

His favourite passage in the Bible was the poetic expression of the prophet Isaiah in Chapter 35. To Flynn this passage was like a bush ballad, declaring that the desert would bloom again. The words inscribed on the plaque embedded in the base of his grave are an echo of this passage:

> He brought gladness and rejoicing to the wilderness and solitary places.

That famous chapter also speaks about a new highway called the Holy Way. The prophecy was that the captive Jewish people would return safely to Jerusalem via the Holy Way. Flynn often quoted this verse, for he understood his mission to be on the long winding bush tracks, seeking to bring a new sense of safety to men and women who were brave enough to make their homes beyond the farthest fences.

Holy or not, it was that west track that was to be either his Nemesis or his triumph.

The great test centred around a wireless set.

For years he had dreamed of planes and radio as the chief components in his mantle of safety providing an air and wireless link between doctor and patient. The planes became available with the advent of Qantas, Australia's first airline, but radio experiments in 1924 and 1925 failed miserably. There were mutterings of 'crank', 'idle fantasies', 'time wasting', and Flynn felt himself to be on trial. He was truly in the wilderness. But he hung on, in characteristic fashion, his eyes on his goal, and the turning point came when he enlisted young Alfred Traeger as his wireless expert.

Alf Traeger was the right man. He had an inventive mind — at the age of twelve he had amazed everyone by making his own telephone receiver and transmitter. He was free of ties, he had a hankering to see the outback, and he found it impossible to say 'No' to John Flynn. At the time, Flynn's salary was £360 a year. He paid Traeger £500. It was a typical Flynn investment and money well spent for eventually Alf produced the radio transceiver and pedal generator on which had hung the hopes and dreams of these two men.

But that didn't happen overnight. The year 1925-26 was a nightmarish one for Flynn. He spent most of it in Alice Springs, living in a tin shed. During the crucial wireless experiments that never quite succeeded, he was forced to give his attention to another of his dreams — the building of the Alice Springs nursing home. The wireless experiments had to be deferred and for nine months Flynn worked shoulder to shoulder with the carpenters and labourers in the construction of the nursing home. He helped cart 80 tonnes of ironwood logs for the lime kiln, necessary for the making of mortar for the thick stone walls. The whole building operation was full of frustrations. All supplies had to come by camel team, a slow 640 kilometre journey from Oodnadatta, the rail head; and the grim spectre of never enough money was ever present. Added to this, it was a long, hot summer and lines of communication with the Board in Sydney were vulnerable to misunderstanding. And all that time, Flynn was aching to get on with the dearest of his dreams — the aerial medical experiments.

At last, however, the building was completed and stood impressively in the small township. While Flynn had had professional help in the preparation of working drawings, the overall design was his brainchild. People who have lived in it commmend it for its coolness and comfort. It has been restored in recent years and is now a museum. Right in the heart of Todd Street, visitors flock to see this unique National Trust building — 'Adelaide House,' the forerunner of today's hospital and for 13 years the only hospital in Central Australia.

Alice Springs in 1926.

1926 was a critical year for Flynn in Alice Springs. In addition to the urgent wireless experiments he had to oversee the building of the Nursing Home.
The Home was opened on June 26, 1926 and called 'Adelaide House'. It was the outstanding and biggest building in the town. The engine room at the rear was used by John Flynn and Alf Traeger as their wireless base for experiments with Hermannsburg and Arltunga.

But back in 1926 Flynn had become dispirited and was losing weight; the set-backs were a burden, and he was aware of increasing criticism from Sydney concerning spending more money on the wireless experiments.

Then, most unexpectedly, the sun burst through the clouds once more. The H.V. McKay Charitable Trust gave him £2,000 ($4,000 — a big sum in those days) towards the aerial medical work. Flynn was now able to proceed with his greatest dream. And that was when Alf Traeger proved himself a splendid investment.

In a letter to his father, on 5 November, 1926, Flynn wrote:

... We have had a strenuous time, but Mr Traeger is very keen indeed and knows his work. We have brought up so much extra gear that it is possible to do what could not be done before. Our generating plant works beautifully and the Home (nursing home) is very bright at night ...
Tomorrow we go out 70 miles over to Hermannsburg, to set up a field station there. After that we go 70 miles east to Arltunga to put one there. They are simple sets which should easily work with this one ...
It looks as if the experiments are going to succeed this time, and open up the way for much expansion.

So it was with high hopes that Flynn and Traeger, that day in November 1926, loaded the heavy duty batteries, aerials and

The MacDonnell Ranges   41

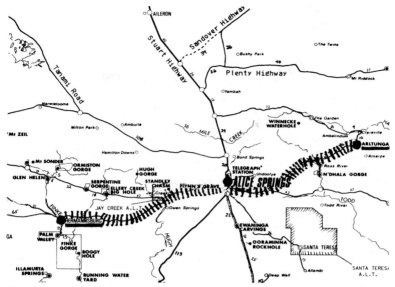

John Flynn's 'wireless highway' to Hermannsburg and Arltunga as he and Alf Traeger battled with radio experiments. On the Hermannsburg track they would regularly pass the very site where Flynn's grave was eventually built.

radio gear in the back of the Dodge Buckboard, and set out west for Hermannsburg. That was when the western road became like the holy highway seen by the prophet.

At the Alice Springs end, in the engine room behind the nursing home, they had installed transmitting and receiving units. The plan was to attempt morse-code communication to and fro between the two centres.

The great moment came early next morning when Traeger tapped out his morse-code message to Alice Springs. He tapped it out again and again, and absolutely nothing happened. 8AB in Alice Springs could not be raised.

Dejected and disappointed, the two men returned to Alice Springs, after arranging another trial schedule for that evening. Pastor Albrecht and Mr Heinrich were to operate the Hermannsburg end.

In Alice Springs hopes were restored, for they discovered that the volunteer operator there, a local policeman, had tuned in on the wrong frequency!

The crisis passed, and at 5 p.m. that day, the miracle happened. Messages were sent and received. The wireless worked. The bush

This is how John Flynn travelled up and down 'the highway' to Hermannsburg in 1926. Note the poles for wireless aerials on the side of the Dodge Four, and the pulley on the rear wheel for working a portable generator. This famous vehicle was used by Alf Traeger in Cloncurry in 1929–33 for installing pedal sets in the Gulf Country. It was eventually sold to Mr Jack Thomas, the bookkeeper at Corinda Cattle Station, for £60 on November 1, 1933.

would be dumb no longer — at last the inlanders were going to have a voice of their own. Out of a nightmare year had come the fulfillment of Flynn's greatest dream.

Within twenty months, Alfred Traeger had manufactured six of his miracle transceivers, each equipped with ingenious pedal generators to provide power for transmitting messages. Cloncurry, in far-west Queensland was selected as the pioneering base for both the first Flying Doctor and the new radio network. A social revolution was afoot in the outback and the radio-medical-aviation 'mantle of safety' was a glorious reality, expanding rapidly year after year.

Hermannsburg Mission

Hermannsburg understandably meant much to Flynn. He and its superintendent Rev. F.W. Albrecht had a lot in common, and Flynn was a frequent visitor at the Mission which was part of pioneering history itself. It was established in 1877 by two German Lutheran missionaries, W.F. Schwarz and A.H. Kempe.

These two men set out from the south in their covered wagon, with horses, sheep and cattle. The contingent moved slowly north but met trouble in the form of a severe drought, forcing them to remain at Dalhousie Springs, near the Northern Territory border, for nearly a year. Those men really suffered — the drought, the

As a result of the successful radio experiments at Hermannsburg in November 1926 Alfred Traeger, still working as Flynn's Radio Engineer, set up a small workshop in Marryatville Adelaide and in two years produced six so-called 'Traeger Transceivers' powered by pedal generators. This started the revolution in communication in the outback and by 1934 there was a widespread network of 'pedal sets' in daily operation as an integral part of Flynn's Flying Doctor Scheme at Cloncurry.

heat, the flies, the problems with their animals all took a great toll. It was only their extraordinary faith and stamina which saw them through.

Battling on, they decided to settle beside the Finke River — that mighty sometimes flooded, but nearly always dry river that has its headquarters near Glen Helen, then winds snake-like through the desert, only to fizzle out in the Simpson. Some of the first buildings erected there remain at the site today.

It took the two missionaries some months to make contact with the Aborigines they had come to serve, but the fact that they

Not only did Alf Traeger invent the miraculous Transceiver for use in homesteads but he also produced portable pedal sets for padres and travellers on the road. This portable pedal set used by Fred McKay while a patrol padre with John Flynn in now housed as a valuable museum item in the National Library Canberra and after 50 years it still works!

remained there at Hermannsburg for 13 years, and that the place is a strong Aboriginal community today, is a tribute to their pioneering achievement.

Schwarz and Kempe made many forays into the interior where no white man had been, and were in fact the first Europeans to see the wonders of Palm Valley.

The historic mission church was dedicated on Christmas Day 1897 during the ministry of Rev. Carl Strehlow, father of T.G.H. Strehlow, a noted authority on Central Australian Aborigines. Carl Strehlow was appointed in 1894 and remained at Hermannsburg for 28 years. Apart from arduous duties at the mission, he studied the Aranda language and wrote a large work on the myths, songs and social organisation of the West Aranda and the Kukatja people. As he came to know the Aborigines, his respect for their culture increased. Not surprisingly he was both respected and loved by them.

In 1922 Rev. Strehlow became seriously ill and in October had a nightmare journey towards medical help. He was taken by buggy over rocky roads, dry river beds, dust and sand, in scorching October heat. Although the few people along the way, both black and white, did their best to help, the journey was unsuccessful, and Carl Strehlow died at Horseshoe Bend.

Rev. F.W. Albrecht took over in 1926 and he too had a long and significant ministry, carried on later by his son Paul.

Hermannsburg, like other mission communities which have now been handed back to the Aborigines, has had its trials and successes, but today is looked on as one of the centres that offers great hope for the future of its people.

Artist Albert Namatjira was born and educated there, and John Flynn came to know him well. Perhaps it was Namatjira, perhaps one of the others at Hermannsburg, who told him the story of the Dingo Dreaming.

The Dingo Trail

John Flynn's grave is close to the Dingo Trail, a story that comes from the Aranda Dreaming. The people believe that their Dingo Spirit ancestors came bounding out of the Simpson Desert and along the main range of the MacDonnells. The huge dingo leader stopped at Mt Gillen's peak and sniffed around; the tip of Mt Gillen is seen by the Aranda people as his nose. He then spied a litter of fat, white puppies below the mountains and leapt down to kill them. Their remains can be seen in the white quartz outcrops on the southern side of John Flynn's grave and in other rock formations in the area.

Sacrilege: To the discerning ear, the same great dingo might have been howling from Mt Gillen on the night of 31 December, 1969. On that night, four young men, caught up in the revelries of New Year's Eve, hurtled along the westward track in their rattling vehicle, and with paint spray guns sprayed the Devil's Marble on Flynn's grave. Daylight revealed the full extent of their handiwork — the pre-historic rock was now covered in psychadelic colours like an over-embellished Easter egg!

The howling of the mythical dingo was nothing compared with the howling of the people of Alice Springs. It seemed as if the entire population had leapt out of their New Year beds and risen up in anger. The sacrilegious act resounded in press and radio all over the land. Local people immediately offered a reward of $500 for the arrest of the culprits. The four young revellers were duly found and charged; all had been drunk. But convicting them did not repair the damage. Although the locals did all they could with wire brushes, hydrochloric acid, paint thinning compounds and every other cleaning agent they could think of, their efforts were fruitless.

There was nothing for it but to take up an offer by Ted Smith to sandblast the Marble. Rev. Fred McKay telegramed him: 'Please proceed urgently with sand-blasting operation to remove outer skin of boulder.' It was drastic action.

So today the Devil's Marble looks different from when George Nichols transported it down the Stuart Highway. It has lost its weathered, red-brown look and now presents a clean-looking grey granite surface. Perhaps the dingo will continue to growl until the passing years restore the Marble to its former dignity.

In the meantime, the symbolism of the dingo-nose peak of Mt Gillen standing guard over the grave of John Flynn, is surely significant. Both are sacred places, in their own way, and to walk there between them feels like walking on holy ground.

The calm serenity of both is shared by all passers-by, whether black or white, bushman or tourist.

Chapter Five

Trail Blazers in the Area

'The only safe shot is the path of danger'
(Flynn 'The Inlander' 1918)*

The people of the outback, for whom John Flynn had such concern, would not have been there were it not for the early explorers, the trail blazers who opened up the country. The MacDonnell Ranges are rich in such history and walking in them is like walking through the past.

John McDouall Stuart
The first white man to set foot on the MacDonnells was one of our greatest early explorers, John McDouall Stuart, an intrepid Scot. He had been in Australia only six years when, at the age of 29, he was chosen as a member of Charles Sturt's 1844 expedition into the Centre. The harsh conditions of the Stony Desert and the seemingly endless, burning sandridges of the Simpson, forced this expedition to turn back. Out of the failure, however, was born McDouall Stuart's determination to lead such an exploration himself. Sixteen years later, his ambition was realised, and his journals make fascinating reading.

Like many others, Stuart was itching to solve the mystery of the centre of the Continent. Was it all just wilderness? All desert? Could it be hiding an inland sea? Was there a lush paradise just waiting to be discovered, another Garden of Eden? Spurred on by a Government promise of £2,000 for the first one to explore the country from south to north, Stuart prepared for his onslaught.

On his first major attempt, he had no Government support. Two patrons, Finke and Chambers, gave him his only financial backing. This was in great contrast to the well equipped

Government sponsored Burke and Wills expedition which was setting out from Victoria on the same mission of crossing the continent. Stuart's starting point was from his own State, South Australia.

He had only two companions with him, Kekwik and Head, on this 1860 foray into the Centre; 13 horses completed the party. Plodding through sandy country they came across a dramatic sandstone landmark, a pillar rising 33 metres in height and six metres in width. Stuart named it Chambers Pillar after his patron and friend. This freak monolith, so well known to Australians today, became a meeting place for people following in Stuart's footsteps as it provided an ideal place to camp and leave messages.

The next place Stuart named was the Finke River, honouring his other patron. He did not realise it at the time, but he had discovered the river thought to be the oldest in the world.

Trudging on, he came to the MacDonnells and, like Flynn fifty years later, he looked with wonder on the ancient hills which he named the MacDonnell Ranges after the Governor of South Australia.

On April 22, he recorded the dramatic statement that has found its way into the pages of Australian history books: 'Today I find by my observations of the sun that I am now camped in the centre of Australia'. He named the spot Central Mt Sturt, in honour of his old leader, Charles Sturt, but this was later changed to Central Mt Stuart. He and his men built a cairn there, left a message in a bottle, raised the flag, and gave three cheers. Somewhat ironically, his journal reads: 'and may it [the flag] be a sign to the natives that the dawn of liberty, civilisation and Christianity is about to break upon them.'

The Aborigines apparently thought differently. They certainly made their protest. On June 16, 1860, that small party of weary men, Stuart, Kekwik and Head, with lean food supplies, badly burnt faces, malnourished bodies and exhausted horses, came face to face suddenly with a large group of hostile Aborigines. Stuart tried friendly overtures, but was unsuccessful. The natives threw boomerangs, and Stuart's men were forced to fire over their heads in an attempt to scare them off. The Aborigines scattered, but came back and attacked again. Deciding it was time to give up, Stuart reluctantly took advantage of the dark night to catch up with their horses that had bolted in terror. The party headed south, arriving home three months later in tatters and emaciated, and with Stuart suffering miserably from eye trouble. Only eight of the 13 horses had survived.

But Stuart was indomitable. Three months later he set out again, following his old tracks to the Finke and over the MacDonnell

Ranges. Still success eluded him. It wasn't until his sixth try in all, in 1862, that he was finally victorious. By that time, the Government had realised he was well worth financial backing, and so he had been able to start out with better equipment. It was July 25, 1862 when his party reached Chambers Bay on the north coast. He attached the flag to the highest tree he could find, and let the cool waters of the Timor Sea wash over him.

The journey home was even more rugged than the forward one, a nightmare of physical effort. Stuart himself was close to death when he was carried back to safety on a stretcher. He had lost the sight of one eye and was greatly emaciated, but he had achieved his great ambition, even though there was no enchanting inland sea to discover. The Overland Telegraph Line is a fine memorial to him, for it was he who blazed the track both for it and the Stuart Highway.

The Burke and Wills expedition actually reached the north coast before Stuart, but their exploration did not achieve as much, and tragically they never returned to tell the story.

Overland Telegraph Line

Other trailblazers through the Centre were the men who built the Overland Telegraph Line.

Stuart's achievements enabled Charles Todd to forge a further link in Australia's history, when he and his men completed the almost unbelievable task of establishing the Overland Telegraph.

Charles Todd was Postmaster General of South Australia when he was charged with responsibility that was mind boggling! Yet he was the right man, for he had been advocating the building of an overland telegraph as far back as 1859. He had already overseen the building of South Australia's first telegraph, and had surveyed the route between Adelaide and Melbourne on horseback.

It was a colossal undertaking. The line had to stretch for 3,218 kilometres, much of it over wild country seen only by John McDouall Stuart and his men, apart, of course, from the Aboriginal tribes who looked on it as their own country. The plan was to complete the task in three sections — north, south and central. Todd had to gather together workmen, food, goods, medical equipment, replacement supplies; to decide where to set up base camps as depots; to organise the droving of sheep to the various centres; to find the necessary teams of bullocks, horses and camels; and to be prepared for all the hidden requirements and emergencies that might arise.

It was necessary to know the whereabouts of trees to cut for poles, and water for men and stock. So Todd decided to send out a survey and reconnaissance party to go ahead of the construction

50   Flynn's Last Camp

team. John Ross, a tall, rugged, black-bearded Scot, was chosen as leader. His written orders from Todd were handed to him on July 7, 1870 and were meticulous. He would have no doubt whatever as to what was expected of him, and he was to return to base at Mt Margaret by mid-September. A surveyor was appointed as second in command, and Ross chose the other three in the party. One of these was Alfred Giles, brother of famous explorer, Ernest Giles. The job description Ross gave to Alfred included the insistence that he must be 'sound of wind and limb', and able to live on corn beef and damper.

Preparations went ahead, and work on the line started on September 15, 1870. Trees were chopped and poles erected for mile after weary mile. The rate of progress was 20 to a mile. Then came the wiring party. Their job was to string the line from pole to pole across mostly never-never country. The section from Port Augusta for 800 kilometres north, went according to schedule and was completed by the due date, January 1, 1872.

But the northern party was in trouble. They had strung up only the first 160 kilometres when the wet season descended on them 'like a wolf on the fold'. Nature excelled herself that year, turning on daily monsoonal downpours. Conditions became intolerable, and when the men became ill in increasing numbers, the work had to stop. That was at the 360 kilometre mark.

Todd sent his Assistant Engineer-in-Chief, Patterson, to the rescue. He left Melbourne with five ships in August 1871 and sailed up to the Roper Bar where he set up a depot — 144 kilometres upstream from the river's mouth. Work then proceeded.

Eventually, after two years of adventure, illness, deaths, troubles and delays, the last of the 37,000 poles was cut and erected, and the vital wire linked up.

The ends met on August 22, 1872 at Frew's Ponds. It was an epic achievement, and in Adelaide there was great rejoicing. A half-holiday was declared and bells rang and flags flew. The small colony had good reason to be proud, for a new era in communication had begun. The outside world was now in Australia, for the Overland Line was linked at Darwin with the submarine cable from England.

Charles Todd heard the news when camped with his men at Central Mt Stuart, just 13 years after the flag had been raised there. Todd's joy was unbounded. His faith in the project was vindicated. Although it was a bitterly cold night, and the men extremely weary, they stayed up late receiving messages of congratulation, and transmitting their replies. They had made world-wide history in the field of both national and international communication.

Charles Todd was knighted for his outstanding achievement. The main road and the river that run through Alice Springs both bear his name while the township itself, previously known as Stuart, was changed to its present name, after Todd's wife Alice.

Francis James Gillen

The men who worked the twelve repeater stations on the Overland Telegraph Line were trail blazers too, playing an important role in our history. Perhaps none was more significant than Francis James Gillen who came first as a line operator to the Centre, then was appointed Post and Telegraph Master at the Alice Springs telegraph station in 1892, a position he held for seven years.

Born at Clare, South Australia, in 1855, Gillen spent his boyhood climbing the Adelaide hills with Aboriginal friends. He was fascinated by the glimpses he had of their culture and determined to learn all he could about these people who seemed to know so many of Nature's secrets.

Gillen became a postal assistant at the age of 12. A few years later when he was asked to go to Alice Springs as a line operator, he was overjoyed. He fell in love with the country, and now, instead of climbing Adelaide hills with the boys, he climbed the MacDonnell Ranges with Aranda men. He took every opportunity to pursue his hobby of studying the culture, and diligently learned the language. Gradually he amassed a great deal of both knowledge and understanding, and was as efficient an anthropologist as he was a telegraphist.

The Aranda people called him 'Oknirrabata', meaning something like great teacher, wise man or big father. They respected him highly and gladly shared their way of life with him.

When Walter Baldwin Spencer, Professor of Biology at Melbourne University, came to Central Australia with the Horn Expedition, he was invited to stay at the Gillen home. He wrote: 'On the occasion of my first visit in 1894, I made my home at the Telegraph Station, and since the day I was welcomed by Mr and Mrs Gillen, there is no part of Australia with which I have had more pleasant or more interesting associations.'

Spencer and Gillen discovered that they were kindred souls, and came to share a lasting working friendship which resulted in an important understanding of Aboriginal culture. Their jointly published books, now pioneering classics, are still studied and highly regarded. Gillen, already so knowledgeable about the Aranda people, was immensely helpful to Spencer in his

Flynn's Last Camp

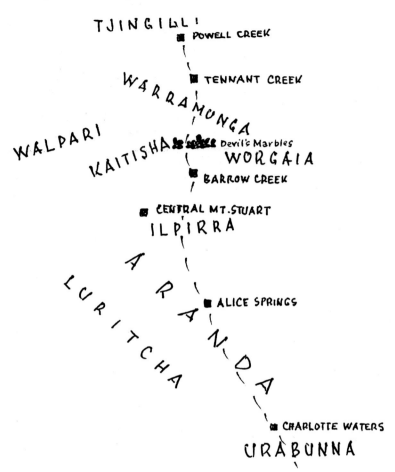

THE SOCIAL GROUPINGS OF ABORIGINAL PEOPLE OF
CENTRAL AUSTRALIA AS VISITED AND STUDIED BY
PROFESSOR W. BALDWIN SPENCER AND MR. F.J. GILLEN
1894-1910

From Alice Springs to Tennant Creek Spencer claims that the Aboriginal Tribes lived in a significantly harmonious relationship anthropological work. The professor invited Gillen to join forces with him in studying the tribes of the Centre and further north, and as a result they worked together for over a decade.

Gillen's health dogged him in the early part of this century and he died in Adelaide in 1912 at the age of only 57. But he left behind him a fine record, particularly in the area of racial understanding.

Author Frank Clune records that it was Charles Winnecke, another Centralian explorer, who named Mt Gillen. The beautiful, inspiring peak of the MacDonnell Ranges is a fitting sentinel over John Flynn's Grave, as it was a much loved landmark for Flynn when ever he travelled along that road leading west.

---

* Flynn founded and, between the years 1913-29, was editor, of *The Inlander*, an illustrated bush periodical with a wide circulation. He also published a quarterly magazine *The Outback Battler* in 1911-12.

Chapter Six

A Proud and Ancient Race

'A man is his friends'
(one of Flynn's proverbs)

Out of the Dreaming
The Aborigines with whom Gillen became so closely associated were from the Aranda tribe whose large tract of country included the Alice Springs and MacDonnell Ranges areas. John Flynn's grave is in this country. A photograph in the National Library shows some of the people helping him load ironwood logs for the lime pits when the Australian Inland Mission nursing home was being built in Alice Springs. The logs were used to stoke the fires in the pits where local stone was burnt to provide lime used as mortar.

The Aranda tribe comes from a proud and ancient race. They have been in Australia for at least 40,000 years, and in all that time they lived in harmony with the land. There was little geological change in Australia during those centuries, so their lifestyle remained much the same. They were nomadic — they had to be because there were no native plants to cultivate, no native animals to herd or domesticate. So such skills as pottery and agriculture were never developed.

But the Aborigines had other abilities. Their sense of sight, hearing, smell and touch became honed to a fine degree; their kinship structures were intricate and efficient; their languages were beautifully constructed; and their social life balanced and secure. Their 'houses' — wiltjas — were necessarily temporary structures and were made from branches and spinifex, easy to erect when camp was made. Within the camp, these wiltjas had a set order, arranged according to kinship structures.

Their nomadic lifestyle meant that they had to limit their possessions to what they could carry. Men bore their spears and other hunting equipment, women their babies, digging sticks and bark receptacles for food. Families, of necessity, had to be limited too.

Men's work was the skilful making of tools and weapons, the hunting for food, the guardianship of the tribe's sacred objects and ceremonies, decision making, and the passing on of tribal lore.

Women's work was the care of small children, food gathering and small game hunting with their dogs, the continuation of female 'ceremonial traditions', the carrying of the precious firesticks, and the preparation of food such as grinding seed for a kind of flour.

Like people everywhere, they had their strengths and weaknesses. They killed each other in inter-tribal wars and had strict punishment laws, including death, within their own groups. Their life was crude, and some of their customs would be distasteful to the average European, but their strong sense of kinship and great affinity for the land surpassed most modern European standards. Such values also ensured the survival of the race and the well-being of the natural environment. When the First Fleet arrived in 1788, it found a continent unharmed by their 40,000-year long presence. At that time, it is estimated there were probably about 300,000 Aborigines living in Australia.

The Aranda, in common with other tribes, believe that the whole earth was originally a dark, bare, flat surface. Underneath that surface, totemic ancestors were sleeping. Time began when these spirit ancestors rose from their sleep, their waking places marked by water holes, special rocks, hills and other natural features.

After their waking, the mythological ancestors, male and female, wandered over the earth, filling it with the plants and animals of their particular totem. They created more physical features as they travelled; in fact, every landscape feature was associated with their deeds or their wanderings. From these same ancestors came the rituals, laws and beliefs that make up the tribal lore. Because they believe that their land is a direct and sacred gift to them from their ancestors, the people are bound, spiritually and inextricably, to their particular country.

So the traumas the Aranda suffered when their land was taken over, can only be imagined. They had hunted and gathered food in and around the MacDonnell Ranges for centuries. The water holes were their own spirit places, from whence they had come and to where they would return. They had rested and camped under the white ghost gums. They had been part of the dawn mists, the thunder storms, the clouds of red dust blotting out the sun, the still heat of summer, the intense cold of winter nights. They had been one with the smell of campfire smoke in the evenings, with the clumps of spinifex dotting the sand, with the daytime bush sounds, and with the overwhelming silence of the night. They had performed their sacred ceremonies, danced to the rhythm of the clapsticks, passed on their traditions, and closely guarded both sacred objects and rituals.

Then came white man with his magic. The Aranda people watched with awe, as Todd's men erected pole after pole and strung the kilometres of wires during the construction of the Overland Telegraph Line. At first they thought it was some kind of fence, and laughed at the stupidity of white man who thought that would keep anything out! They were terrified when they saw horses and camels and bullocks for the first time, then they grew resentful as they watched these same animals drinking from their precious, sacred waterholes, and eating the good pastures of their hunting grounds. White man felt justified in shooting kangaroos, but if an Aranda man killed a horse or bullock for food, he was shot.

At that time there were few restrictions on settlers who took up large areas of land for farming or grazing. Every settlement, of course, meant less hunting ground, but more devastating than this was the loss of land the people had thought was theirs and was sacred to them. Then, with the increasing number of white male settlers in a country where few white women dared to go until well into this century, Aboriginal women and girls became vulnerable; part-Aboriginal babies compounded the problem as there was no place for them in the ancient kinship structure. Then came white man diseases against which the Aboriginal people had no immunity. Epidemics such as influenza and measles took a great toll of life.

Those who tried to retaliate were powerless against the might and magic of the white race, and little by little, the Aborigines retreated. There was no compensation, no contract of sale, no recognition of any rights. Government nominated Protectors were appointed, and Crown land set aside for the establishment of Aboriginal reserves. Gradually the people were given a kind of paternal protection on these reserves or on the mission settlements conducted by the churches. Some opted to take their family groups to cattle stations where a few were employed and all kept in food and varying degrees of care.

Tribal life was dislocated. They were cut off from their spiritual land, bewildered, lost and despairing. Their culture was badly fractured. Poetess Mary Gilmore expressed it this way:

> We were the lost who went,
> Like the cranes, crying;
> Hunted, lonely and spent;
> Broken and dying.

In the last two decades, white Australians have been more conscious of the plight of the Aborigines, and consultation with recognised tribal leaders has opened up new avenues of hope for the people. The Government has responded in significant ways. As a result of the Woodward Commission, appointed in 1974, the Aboriginal Land Rights (N.T.) Act was passed in 1976. This enabled Aborigines to gain title to existing reserves, and to lay claims for traditional areas of land. The Act provided for Aboriginal Land Councils, and the Central one is the one to which the Aranda people relate.

Of further significance is the outstation movement whereby Aboriginal clan groups are moving back into the bush to try to revitalise their culture and revive their relationship with the land.

The Government's stated policy is one of self-determination. The road to that goal is a long and difficult one, and during the transitional period the struggle is great. New goals are having to be found for the old ones which have gone, and only the people themselves can make those decisions which determine their future and restore the pride and dignity of their race.

The Aranda Artists

The main art forms of the people in their tribal state were cave painting and carving, and body decoration. The latter was an intricate art in which traditional designs were used by special members of the tribe.

In more recent times, however, the Aranda people have become well known throughout Australia and even beyond, through the water colour paintings of Albert Namatjira. His monument, near Hermannsburg, reads 'This is the landscape that inspired the artist.' It looks out over the country he knew and loved so well, his spirit land which he depicted so beautifully in water colours.

Albert Namatjira (1900-1959): The story of Namatjira is a tragic one. He was a boy when he met the late Rex Battarbee, an artist who was painting in the vicinity of the Hermannsburg Mission Station. Battarbee employed Albert as his camel boy on the understanding that he would lead him to good spots for painting. In return, the artist would teach the young Aborigine to paint. After two months, Rex Battarbee became convinced his pupil

Albert Namatjira. The track past the John Flynn Grave was also Namatjira's track to Haast Bluff.

would one day be famous. This conviction was justified — people today pay very large sums of money to possess an Albert Namatjira water-colour original.

The tragedy was that although Namatjira won fame for his work, he lost his true identity in the white man's world. He was taken around Australia and put on show along with his paintings. He was wined and dined and introduced to Sydney's night clubs. He rubbed shoulders with the elite and met the Queen. This was the man who, in between his art shows down south, sat on the red sand, paint brush in hand, ants crawling over his body, flies bothering his face, and wife Rubina near by looking for bush tucker. He lived in two worlds and was an oddity in both. The granting of civic rights as a special honour (Aboriginal people did not have them at that time), served only to alienate him further from his puzzled kinsmen — puzzled because traditionally they shared everything.

Broken in spirit, a conversation piece in white society and not understood by his own people, Namatjira died in utter loneliness in 1959 before he was sixty years old.

Other native water-colour artists, through the Aranda School of Water-Colourists, have attempted to follow in the steps of the master, meeting with varying degrees of success. These have included Albert's sons — Enos, Oscar, Ewald, Keith and Maurice — his grandson, Gabriel, and others such as the Pareroultjas, Ebataringas, Pankas, Raberabaras, Landara, Rantje and many more. Often their ability has been sacrificed to the need for quick cash. Tragically the same sadness has been evident in the lives and deaths of many of them.

John Flynn and the Aborigines

The year that Gillen died, 1912, was the year when John Flynn was in the Centre and North, compiling two reports which he presented to the Church on his return. The first one, on the needs of settlers, resulted in the formation of the Australian Inland Mission. The second, on the needs of the Aboriginal people he observed, was fated to fade into oblivion. This was perhaps because the Church's Mission Department had initiated a move of its own to find out the needs of Aborigines. A young school teacher, J.R.B. Love was sent out the following year 'for the purpose of enquiring into the conditions of life among the Aborigines of the Interior'. Love himself later, as an ordained minister, helped with the establishment of Ernabella Mission in Central Australia. He and John Flynn were close friends, their letters to each other revealing the depth of their concern for the people of the Inland, both black and white.

In Flynn's Aboriginal report, he urged the Church to do something to uplift and champion the cause of 'a race that is despised by the whites of this country, but that is probably the most interesting of all savage races at present in existence, and a race that has at least the germs of some of the finest qualities, if it also exhibits some pitiful degradation.'

This attitude must have been almost revolutionary back in 1912 when most Australians regarded Aborigines as wild animals or at best simple children. In 1913 Flynn went on to say that the Church would not carry conviction until it did something for Aboriginal people. Then in 1915 he declared that Aborigines had a right to increasing opportunities for self-development. It wasn't until 60 years later, in 1972, that the Commonwealth Government echoed these words 'self-development'. In 1927 Flynn came out strongly again with the statement:- 'We Australians who, lightheartedly, for four generations have been reading to Aborigines the 'move aside clause' will surely be called up to

Bobbie Meyers, proud friend of John Flynn, who worked as Carpenter's Assistant right through the building contract on the Memorial Church.

render an account of our stewardship. God only knows how soon.'

Prophetic words indeed, yet each time he championed the cause of the Aborigine, he was besieged by critics who felt that already too much was being done for 'a dying race'. Some, however, believed that much more should be done, particularly in the nursing homes. Flynn gave careful thought to this matter. In 1932 he wrote:

> As regards care of the blacks. In my opinion a 'public hospital' would not be satisfactory. If they are to be treated with due consideration, their patients must be permitted to be visited by their friends. If they are to be made comfortable they should be given special beds,

practically on the ground. In fact for 'camp blacks' their hospital, whilst truly sanitary, should be designed to serve children of the open air. The Staff, too, should be mission sisters specially devoted to Aborigines — devoted enough to study their language and habits of thought . . . The Aborigines of Central Australia deserve specialised care in their own institution at the hands of sisters who are consecrated to their particular cause.

Obviously Flynn was concerned with the practical problems. By the 'visiting of friends' he meant the whole family group who would accompany the sick person to hospital, camp on the spot and require food. He was also aware of the fact that, in those days, it would be a rare Aborigine who could bear to be on a bed, under a roof. He would feel most insecure.

John Flynn had neither the money at his disposal, nor the mandate to directly take on the problems of the Aboriginal people. However, there is no gainsaying that their plight was always of grave concern to him; it comes through in his private letters to friends, in his public statements to Church and Community leaders and in his publications — the first issue of the 1915 *Inlander* was devoted to photographs and stories on the plight of the fringe-dwellers in particular. It is not unfitting therefore that his last resting place should be in Aranda territory.

Footnote: The fact that John Flynn was commissioned by the Church in 1912 to pioneer a practical ministry to the isolated white population of the outback made it imperative for him to concentrate on this specially defined task. Controversy arose in the period 1934-36, and was revived again in 1972, when claims were made that he should have given more concentrated attention to the social conditions of the Aboriginal people. However, Flynn was never deflected from pursuing the particular goals he had set 'to make family life safe and happy in the lonely frontier areas' and the public controversy which arose actually helped in the end to clarify some understandable misapprehensions about the unique role he was fulfilling. Details of this controversy are documented in the official records within the National Library, Canberra.

Chapter Seven

On the Move in the Centre

'The Aborigine has a great secret; he knows when to go walkabout!'
(Flynn in a roadside camp 1937)

Transport
The Aborigines would have arrived in Australia with the aid of canoes. Since then they had only one other form of transport — their feet. For thousands of years their feet took them wherever they wanted to go on land.

Then came the first white men with their horses and bullocks, which quickly proved unsatisfactory at covering the long, hot, waterless distances of the Outback.

And so the camel came into its own.

When John Flynn rode into Alice Springs on the back of a camel, he was using a common means of transport.

Australia owes much to both camels and drivers, for it was they who plodded through the Centre, year in, year out, carrying the much needed supplies of outback pastoralists and remote mining communities such as Hatches Creek and Tennant Creek. When loaded, it took the camel team four months to go from Oodnadatta, the railhead, to Newcastle Waters, then, unloaded, three months for the return journey.

Thomas (later Sir Thomas) Elder, a South Australian pastoralist, was convinced that camels were the answer to the Centre's transport problems, and in 1866 he had 121 camels brought out from Karachi. He founded Australia's first camel stud farm at Beltana. This turned out to be a very successful venture, and before long, Elder and his partner, Stuckey, were operating camel

Camel wagon, 70 miles south of Alice Springs, with load of building material for construction of Alice Springs Nursing Home.

teams throughout Central Australia. Some of the drivers came from Afghanistan, but most of them were from northern India and what is now West Pakistan, but all were known as Afghans or just Ghans.

The camels certainly proved themselves. They carried mail, food stuffs, building materials, in fact anything that was needed. Charles Winnecke, the explorer, made an epic journey of over 400 kilometres through the sand-ridged Simpson Desert, and his camels, some of them carrying very heavy loads, walked for 16 days in blistering heat without a drink. After a one day rest, they plodded on for a further 240 kilometres without water.

The camels helped make themselves redundant by carrying supplies for the construction of the Central Australian railway. The line progressed by fits and starts between the years 1879 to 1929 when it finally reached Alice Springs, bearing the train that came to be known affectionately as 'The Ghan'. The camel legs gave way to wheels, but the name remained to remind people of the sterling contribution the teams made in the inland.

Then came an increasing number of road vehicles, improving as the years went by.

Kurt Johannsen's unique transport system out of Alice Springs was the forerunner to the great road trains that thunder down the Stuart Highway today. Kurt had a regular mail run to various outposts, and often brought back bales of wool or other cargo as return loading. His vehicles were noted for their hybrid character; one he used in 1936 combined a Dodge Differential with a Willys Knight chassis and a Buick engine!

Today the fast freight trains, the great road trucks and the cargo planes have all replaced the camel, but this extraordinary animal still has its uses. Tourists like to experience the rocking motion of a camel ride, and the annual Camel Derby is a magnet for visitors to the Centre. There is a camel farm in Alice Springs, while the wild descendants of those released by the camel drivers years ago can sometimes be seen wandering the bush, to the delight of the tourist lucky enough to catch a glimpse. Astonishingly too, there are still places that only a camel can negotiate. For instance, an Aboriginal child attending a college in Darwin returned to his home in Central Australia via jet to Alice Springs, coach to a point on the south road, and from there completed his journey across the rough terrain on the back of a camel.

In front of the Alice Springs Civic Centre there stands a monument to the Afghan drivers to whom this country owes so much. John Blakeman, for many years manager of the A.I.M. Old Timers' Homes persistenly pressed for such a memorial. John was a long standing admirer of these Afghans and became a friend to several of their descendants. He also keeps alive their memory.

White People are Nomads too

It is only a short step from transport to tourism. The trail Stuart's horses blazed through the MacDonnells is now, a century later, a busy tourist route. The Aborigines are not the only ones with an urge to roam or go walkabout. White man too is a kind of nomad.

All year long visitors pour into Alice Springs. They come in planes, coaches, trains, cars, caravans and on motor cycles. They come in groups, school parties, families or as individuals. In the hot summer months they come in organized tours from the northern hemisphere winters, then from May to September there is a kind of tourist lemming rush from the south.

What is it that calls all these visitors to Central Australia? Is it the bargain-packaged tour? Is it a mystique, in the bones since childhood — a longing to leave the concrete city behind, to experience the 'real' Australia? Is it perhaps a hangover from pioneer ancestors, a yearning for a frontier existence?

Whatever the reason, the magnet is there, and thousands of tourists come each year to fulfil their own particular dream. Perhaps it is a longing for purification and regeneration, such as the Aborigines experience in their renewing ceremonies.

A Pioneer of Tourism in Central Australia

Len Tuit pioneered tourism in the Northern Territory. An article in the *Inland Review* (Dec. 1968) by Alan Wauchope and Peter English, describes him as 'the father of Centralian tourism'.

In 1932 he arrived in Alice Springs in his truck, and set himself up as a contract driver, transporting goods up and down the rough track between Alice Springs and Tennant Creek. By 1936 he had

On the Move in the Centre 65

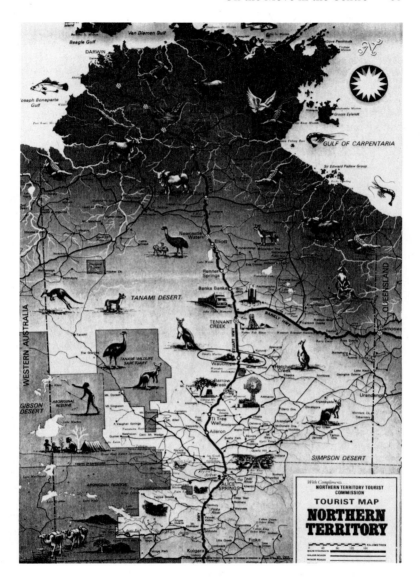

acquired a new Ford truck, and expanded his business to the isolated goldfields at the Granites and Tanami, way out in the lonely desert to the north-west.

After the war, he was appointed as official mail carrier between Alice Springs and Darwin. It was then that he began to take passengers on the three days' journey. He charged them about $40 for the all inclusive fare. This, in 1946, was the first regular road passenger service on that route.

Business flourished and Len Tuit's horizons stretched with it. His eye was on Ayer's Rock as a potential tourist target. The authorities and the local public laughed at him. 'There's no future in tourism in the Northern Territory, and Ayer's Rock in particular' they told him. Words they are surely eating today!

Tuit was of John Flynn's mould and didn't give up easily. He took matters into his own hands and in 1950 took a group of 44 students and teachers from Knox Grammar School in Sydney to Ayer's Rock on a ten days' camping expedition. The project was a success, but Tuit could see there could be no more such trips unless water was readily available in the area. He gathered together all the necessary equipment and set out to find that water himself. He struck it at 87 feet. Delighted, he put in the bore, then turned his attention to organising the beginning of the trek of thousands of school parties and tourist groups to the Rock.

The children and staff of those early school camps became enthusiastic ambassadors for the Australian heartland, and Len was able to replace his nine Kombies with conventional coaches, which soon became a regular sight passing through Kulgera and Curtin Springs.

Not content with that success, he turned his sights to Palm Valley and put that on the tourist map too. In 1963 he sold up all his interests and went south. But he found he couldn't stay away, and returned to Alice Springs to conduct a much needed local bus service. His title of 'father of Centralian tourism' was well earned.

Len Tuit was forward-looking, but even he could not have foreseen what his simple beginnings would lead to. The well planned, attractive village of Yulara, 15 kilometres from Ayer's Rock and within easy reach of the Olgas, is a far cry from that first school camp. Yet its excellent range of accommodation from international hotel to comfortable camping, its captivating Visitors' Centre, its provision for tourists' needs, its delightful planning of colour and design to fit in with the desert environment, are all in a way a tribute to Len Tuit who, in spite of opposition, had the vision and followed his dream. Now visitors come from all over the world to see the great monolith and the beauty of the Olgas, and Len Tuit's faith is vindicated.

Today's Tourists

The modern tourist is the inheritor of a great legacy. People like McDouall Stuart, John Ross, Charles Todd, John Flynn, Kurt Johannsen and Len Tuit have all made it possible for today's travellers to share in the unique attractions of the inland. These men didn't see the end results of their work as far as tourism is concerned, but they were the path-finders, the road builders. A poem Flynn often quoted reflects this feeling. It is entitled 'The Master Joy' by Friedlander.

> We shall not travel by the road we make;
> Ere day by day the sound of many feet
> Is heard upon the stones which now we break,
> We shall not come to where the cross-roads meet.
>
> For us, the heat by day, the cold by night,
> The inch slow progress, and the heavy load.
> And death at last to close the long grim fight
> With man and heat and stone; for them the Road.
>
> For them the shade of trees that now we plant,
> The safe, smooth journey, and the final goal,
> Yea, birthright in the land of covenant —
> For us day labour, travail of the soul.
>
> And yet — the road is ours as never theirs!
> Is not one joy on us alone bestowed?
> For us the Master-joy, O Pioneers —
> We shall not travel, but we make the road.

Flynn must have identified significantly with this poem, for he had hundreds printed and distributed.

Thousands of visitors today are able to enjoy the fruits of the road builders, and indulge their own interests of rock hunting, bird watching, photography, painting, exploring, walking or just meditating. More than this, many visitors feel themselves more closely identified with Australia than ever before, returning to their homes with a sense of regeneration.

Chapter Eight

A Prophet in the Wilderness

'Go out and listen!'
(Flynn to new patrol padre, 1935)

John Flynn was one such prophet. He found, like other prophets, that it was in the silence of the desert that visions were nurtured, and life's priorities put into perspective; that in the desert there was no clutter, physical or mental; that out there in the wilderness one was forced back to basics.

His efforts were instrumental in breaking the 'tyranny of distance'. Out of his vision, he tamed distance, putting 'hobbles on the bush' as the old-timer expressed it. In the desert space which had become a hostile enemy, he created small oases of friendly space in the form of his nursing homes, the patrol padres, the pedal wireless sets, the flying doctors. Flynn was a 'spacious' man — his visions reached beyond known horizons.

Desert and wilderness experiences have been important to people throughout history. It was in the wilderness that Moses saw the burning bush and was thrust into his life's work; again where he received the Ten Commandments; it was in the desert that Elijah heard the still small voice of calm; where the Desert Fathers kept the fire of Christianity alive in the second, third and fourth centuries while the world around them was in a state of decadence; where John the Baptist cried out 'Prepare the way of the Lord' and exhorted people to repent of their wrong doings; in the desert where Christ Himself had His loyalty and commitment to God tested.

John Flynn personified this desert spirituality. Many people flee to the desert to escape the desert in their own lives; perhaps they

A tourist party pulls up at the Grave on September 17, 1978 and an open air memorial service is conducted by Rev. Fred McKay, assisted by Rev. Lloyd Shirley, to mark the official unveiling of the Jean Flynn Plaque.

identify with the physical harshness of the wilderness. But Flynn came, not to escape, but to minister to it, and through it, and in it. The very title 'Flynn of the Inland' as he was known throughout Australia, points to this. He was part of the desert, not, like a miner, trying to extract something from it, but always giving himself to it, in a truly serving capacity.

Some might reckon him great because of his accomplishments. But Flynn's true greatness lay in his compassionate, serving heart; in his vision and keen mind that never gave up on problems others deemed too hard to handle; and in his unswerving faith in God and his fellow man.

Robert Browning in his poem 'Asolando' could have been thinking of Flynn when he wrote this:

> One who never turned his back but marched breast forward,
> Never doubted clouds would break,
> Never dreamed, though right were worsted, wrong would triumph,
> Held we fall to rise, are baffled to fight better,
> Sleep to wake.

'There was a man sent from God whose name was John', quoted Skipper Partridge at the ceremony when Flynn's ashes were interred. 'Amen!' echoed the many folk of the outback who had such reason to rejoice that through this man the desert had truly blossomed.

Thoughts that lie too deep for tears.

John Flynn's Last Camp

Five kilometres out from Alice Springs, 80,000 travellers a year pause there on the western road beside the lonely grave. Old friends come like pilgrims to their Mecca, tourists ask questions and photograph it from all angles, artists paint it, and visitors from other countries wonder about the extraordinary gravestone and the man it honours.

Little wonder then, that when the bush people come to Alice Springs and stand before John Flynn's last camp, they have thoughts that lie too deep for tears.

This is a very special grave, in a very special place. Watch over it carefully then, you craggy Mt Gillen, you sentinel ghost gums, you whispering corkwoods, for you are guarding the last camp of one of Australia's great sons.